INFALLIBLE LOVE

by
Lenore

Order this book online at www.trafford.com
or email orders@trafford.com

Most Trafford titles are also available at major online book retailers.

Printed in Victoria, BC, Canada.

ISBN: 978-1-4269-2044-8

*Our mission is to efficiently provide the world's finest, most comprehensive book publishing
service, enabling every author to experience success. To find out how to publish your book, your
way, and have it available worldwide, visit us online at www.trafford.com*

Trafford rev. 12/28/09

 Trafford
PUBLISHING® www.trafford.com

North America & international
toll-free: 1 888 232 4444 (USA & Canada)
phone: 250 383 6864 ♦ fax: 812 355 4082

THIS BOOK IS DEDICATED
TO THE PEOPLE WHO BELIEVE IN ME

ROY AND PEGGY JACKSON
KEVANTE KOREY PRICE
MASON AND JUANITA GORDON
MASON GORDON JR
REGINALD JACKSON
ANTHONY JACKSON
SEBASTIAN
BRONICA DEALE
"PAUL" THE APOSTLE
CHASTITY DAY
JIMMY VALENTINE
WYKENA WHITE
JEREMY SIMON
AND
ALL THE HATERS

TABLE OF CONTENTS:

BLACK WOMAN FROWN
HELP
LEARN WHO YOU'RE DEALING WITH
I OBJECT
IT'S NOT ABOUT YOU
CATER
M'S ETHER
QUIT IT: BOOK II
"A" TO THE LEFT
ODE 2 "B"
DYING BREED
IT'S MY FAULT
PHENOMENAL LENORE

MEN ALL PAUSED

BLIND HELL DATE
MY BAD
LIGHT SKINNED CUTIE
SEX IN THE CITY

I NEED
ALMOST FAMOUS (ODE 2 ED)
RING THE ALARM
DEAR KOREY
DEAR DADDY
MY SON

<u>GOD IS TELLING ME SOMETHING</u>

REASONABLE DOUBTS
CHAPTER ONE
TESTIFY
SOUL CLEANSING
CHANGE
GOD'S APOLOGY
LORD GIVE ME A SIGN
I WAS - I AM
LENORE

WHO, WHAT, WHERE, WHEN AND WHY

STAR DREAMS
HOMELESS
PEP BOYS
CHRYSLER SUCKS
REAL HOUSEWIVES OF ATL?
RADIO AIR PLAY
37
CLOVES
NATURAL HIGH
I MISS YOU

DECEMBER 25TH, 2008

The only thing infallible about me is my love for poetry. My love for words and the strange ways I put them together that make my poems different from any other poet. I kept seeing the word infallible, so this morning I looked through "Webster" to get the exact meaning. I felt as if the word described my exact feelings about poetry. So, I walked into the bathroom with the dictionary, sat on the toilet and became lost in my thoughts. I decided what ever section I opened to; I would choose a word from that page to complete the title. As I looked over the two pages, could it have been a coincidence that I opened the dictionary to the letter "L." All the words on the page didn't make any sense to the feelings I wanted to convey. Except one, Love. Thus "Infallible Love," was born.

I'm amazed at my growth since I published my first book in 2005. More so, I amazed at how I was able to do a complete self actualization and work on everything I wanted to change about myself. Recently, I was giving a co-worker some advise on how to handle a certain situation, when she asked if I was always as strong as I am now. The answer was no, nor am I ashamed of my awful past.

When I moved to Atlanta in 1997, I was just another crazy bitch and a useless soul in society. My mind was gone, and my behavior was unexplainable.

My first book "Undeniably Me," explained how I started to get off the right path mentally which started as a child. I was an angry insecure child that turned me into a bitter black woman.

Yet, I learned that God places certain people in your path that can facilitate your growth or hinder your development forever. I guess I made the right choice.

I've never hidden the fact that I sought professional help, because I realized that I couldn't face my issues alone. Mary-Alice Hines, the best psychologist in "Buckhead." She became the most important woman in my life next to my mother. I was diagnosed as a Co-dependant personality with anger issues and ADHD. I can laugh at it now because my issues are under my control.

The second important factor is my growth were the men that God placed before me. I will call them my D.A. and I'm not talking about an attorney. It's my Dayton-Atlanta click. The strongest group of men I've ever met. I watched, I listened and basically studied them like it was a course in school. They praised me when I did good, and educated me when I made mistakes. They saw potential in me that I never saw in myself. Most importantly, I had book sense, my psychologists helped with common sense, and they brought the street sense.

So, here I am years later and a second chance at my dream, and I finally worked out the major issues. As my mind began to heal, I was no longer oblivious to the mental and physical issues that plagued me for years. Not only did I have to detox my mind, but I had to detox my body.

I couldn't dwell on my problems from the past. I could only concentrate on my future. However, I would solve one problem and another one would arise. I would solve that one, and then something new came up. I began to think it was a vicious cycle that would never end. Yet, I never gave up. I was determined to make my life as normal and as stable as possible.

I didn't have a major break through until I got out of my own way. In life we can sometimes be our own worst enemy, and I wasn't the type of enemy I wanted to have. I never thought about how or when the process would end, I never question God why my upbringing had to hinder me mentally and physically. I just dealt with it. I can look back at the young girl I use to be and just laugh. I love it when I haven't seen people in years and they can't believe the women I've become. I'm proof that people can change, and even when I think I'm at my best, I learn something new about me that can be approved. I'm far from perfect and only strive to be the best person I can. But how do you pause life from going on without you? You can't you have to deal with the good and the bad.

The past few years have been the hardest because God called upon my last parent, my father. I took a few steps backward, well more than a few steps. When I lost my mother I thought, "well at least I have my dad." Yet, until this day I still blame myself for his death. I know he was 300 miles away and there was nothing I could have done.

I wonder if I was a little more selfish with my father, would he still be alive until this day.

I have these dreams a gift of sight in my sleep, that I haven't learned to handle. I saw his death. My mother and I chased down the person responsible. Yet I knew if I mentioned the dream to him, I could risk the fall out from his new family. A part of me died with both of them, and left that part of me in Montgomery and I never looked back.

I started going back to church looking for answers, and God delivered. For a couple of months, I was in church every Sunday. I loved listening to the choir, and I had the perfect spot in the balcony over looking the packed congregation. Although I went to church alone, I never felt alone.

The messages were penetrating my heart and soul, and I even took notes during the sermon. I was already a believer I just needed conformation. I watched this same preacher via television previously and got the same message. The members started to harass me about joining, so I began to sneak out a little early. I knew this congregation experience was coming to an end, and I would return back to my congregation of one, my living room.

On the last Sunday I attended, I was in my normal spot in the balcony right in front of the rail. As we began to pray, I moved to the edge of the pew. I looked down, clasped my hands and closed my eyes. All of the sudden I was at a concert in the back of a crowd, and I couldn't see who was on the stage. I kept jumping up and down trying to see who was performing.

Clouds of smoke bellowed from the ceiling and a bright light caught my attention. Two hands reached out for me, although I couldn't see a face I knew it was God. I started jumping and reaching because I wanted to touch him so badly. I couldn't reach him, yet I didn't give up. Then like an ant these hands so big, so calming and so powerful lifted me by my shoulders and set me on that stage with my back to the crowd. And as quickly as the hands appeared they were gone. I turned around and this crowd was there to see me. It was my show and I felt weak to my knees. I barely caught myself as I almost fell off that pew. Not only was the prayer over, but the young lady next to me looked at me as if I was crazy. Oh, but I'm not crazy. He gave me an opportunity to see what I could have as long as I kept him in sight and reaching for the heavens. True Story.

Here we go again. Many will judge my words as obscene maybe even perverse. Many will hate on me because I choose to speak to the truth. I have no regrets anymore. I was so afraid to die that I didn't live. My only fear is God. He knew the poems I was working on before he gave me that vision. Yet only he knows the bigger plan I have for this earth. So, If I offend anyone by my words, maybe you should take a look inside yourself. Open your mind and let me converse with you for a while. My words speak to the ordinary people. Call me what you want, think of me what you will because I don't care. I'm a poet, artist and a child of God. Guess what, he loves us sinners too.

"Wankster"
A Poetic Story

WANKSTER

When I meet anyone, I give them the benefit of the doubt. I let them bury themselves, with the nonsense coming out of their mouth. Fake it until you make it, was one nigga's motto, but this fake ass gangster will never have bravado. The first time he rhymed for me, I wondered why he stole Jay-Z's flow? The more I watched him he pretended if he had Jigga type of dough.

At work he tried to steal accounts, taking money out of mine and my friends hand. We may have gotten them back but this is when I started to formulate my plan.

One day he came in crying like a little chick. Some nigga disrespected him and he didn't know how to handle it. His emotions were all over the place, stomping and pouting like a little girl. I was embarrassed for him, because he is starting to show his real world. He decided to ask me for my advice, yet this nigga is a gangster, does he really have to think twice? I could see the fear in his eyes, and if he was all alone, I'm sure he would cry. My sick little mind wanted to have some fun, so I ask, how are you a gangster and you don't have a gun? The next week he said he had a gun, well not really, there was a 10 day waiting period for one. I quickly corrected his lie, in the state of Georgia there's no waiting time.

Weeks went by, and everything that came out of his mouth, sounded like a lie. Imaginary situations of stories he told, he needed attention, pretending like his my-space went gold. This dude couldn't be trusted and he was kinda close to a friend of mine. The next time I saw my friend I warned to watch his back, when this dude is within time.

At work he got caught up in his own bullshit. When he was called into the office, he began to fake snitch. I had a friend who wasn't on his robbery game, but when shit got hot his tongue slipped my boys name. When my friend told me how his trouble began, I warned him he wasn't dealing with a real man. A couple of others did the same shit, and while we were on smoke break, wankster acted like he was really legit. Proclaiming his innocence, "that shit and right!" Yea nigga your shit aint right. His twisted mind shuts on and off like a like switch. One more reason I wanted to break down this bitch.

So I kept my enemy close, and like a wankster his secrets he spilled. It's a damn shame, he couldn't see I was the real deal. Did he think I forgot he tried to steal from me. And since he admired my swagger, bringing him down was going to be extra sweet. It helped even more all the enemies he made walking through the door. He should have been fired a long time ago, but his protector hides everything he knows. Plus I knew he wasn't going to get fired. Just a couple of days his cheating would retired. So I dropped some words on the floor, in the right ear I whispered some more.

Yea my intentions could possibly fall, but its the chance you take when you're dealing with the 48 laws. His subterfuge brought him down, and just like a bitch, he started acting like a clown. Once again for two days straight he cried and whined like a little girl, all he was missing was a weave with some pin curls. Truth is, he was mad he could no longer steal and cheat. Yet he was stupid, that while cheating his goal he couldn't meet. Then the look he gave me, he had figured it out. It was to me he spilled his secrets and the one who fucked him no doubt. I looked right back at him with no shame; my eyes read stealing my money was the start of this game.

The chick next me already knew he was a fake a mess. He told her, "she don't know what I would do to her, while sitting at his desk. We looked at each other and laughed it was so absurd. A real gangster would have said it to me, instead of a conversation he wanted over heard. She added, "what kind of boy wants to fight a girl?" Exactly a boy afraid of a grown mans world. I could have had his job, but this nigga was already a miserable slob. Since he wants to add a by the way threat. I'm going to add the finishing touch next. Did he think I was going to let him get that shit off? He thought if he put that in the atmosphere, his words were going to get lost. So I called our so-called mutual friend. I had warned him a month ago this nigga wasn't a real man. Plus this nigga don't know who he dealing with, I'm not a gangster but my inner circle aint no bullshit. Pass this message and tell him I heard his threat, so what ever is going to happen, let it happen next.

An hour or so later, I'm at home meditating trying to enlighten my mind. My cell rings with an unknown number, usually I won't answer but for some reason I'm inclined. No hello, I ask who is this, interrupting my yoga space. In a voice so sweet, it's the wankster wanting to talk about the events of the day. "Click," nigga please I said what I had to say. Come on dude, why do we need to talk about our feelings. Everything in on the table, you confused friendship with business dealings. His ego must have been hurt, because he needed to explain at any cost. Now he's calling my house again, dude you're starting to piss me off. I didn't give him a chance to talk, telling him to never call my house again. As a matter of fact when I hang up, I'm getting in touch with one of my friends. I'm gonna teach this nigga a lesson, and have someone drop him a dime, words from a real gangster, will ring in his ears like his absent "nine."

So I text the "Apostle," I have a problem I need you to solve. The "Apostle," text me back, call me when you're ready to talk. I'll call him shortly with the cause; I need to finish my yoga tape it's on pause.I get another text and it definitely ain't my friend. It's the wankster and he's mad, he's figured out we were never friends. "I hate you, I thought you were cool, how dare you call my friend, you're a two faced bitch don't ever speak to me again."What is dude thinking, I'm the one that told my friend to give him a call, and if he wasn't my friend would he have really got involved?

Would a real man text, don't talk to him again. When I hung up the second time what didn't he understand? I think I need to give him a mental shove, because his text read, like my friend was his love. So I send him, "real gangsters don't send text messages."

He sends one back, "real women don't hang up the phone." Now, I'm on the floor laughing, wishing I was a fly on his wall. The way he is acting, I would love to see that tear drop fall. I'm bored and I want to get back to my yoga tape, I send him simple message, "go away."

Here comes another three page text, a lie so to true. Trying to explain his threat, to late it already left you. "Blah, blah, blah, don't talk to me anymore, blah, say what you want, blah, keep my name out of your mouth, blah, I'm going to keep cheating," But not one threat coming this way. He reminds me of the legally blond dog, bruiser. So I send him one last text, "Loser."

Damn this nigga is texting me again. I didn't even respond because he was a waste of my send, at that point I decided to let my mouth become my pen.

Oh shit, I forgot to call the "Apostle." Together we laughed at the wasted text messages, and assured me if I needed him, he would "XX XXXXX XX XXXXX" a lesson. Nah, I can tell his ego I chopped down. I loved being affiliated with nigga's who don't want to see me frown. Plus I'm over it, and if any one at work finds out, it will be the diarrhea coming from his mouth.

They warned him not to call me, and he should have taken their advice. His bravado didn't match his ego and he couldn't understand that sacrifice. He started running around the job, telling his side of the story, worried I would do it first, but I already had his glory. Of course other losers bought his lie, but these dumb bitches think his broke ass is a gold mine. For two day's everywhere I was he showed up, Sneaking up on my conversations, his insecurities had him fucked up. He hated when people stopped by my desk and speak. He interrupted our conversations about his gangster rap career of the week. I had no reason to converse with him, because as I was concerned we were through. Stupid is as stupid does, and I guess that's what stupid must do.

Still until this day he feels as if he has something to prove, every conversation is about being a gangster and now he wants to be wu tang clan too. One day before break he announces he has to write his cousin in jail. The only thing he can convince me of was his mind was locked in a fake ass gangster cell.

A failure at the job he decided it was time to quit, he announced his last day like he wanted to start some shit. I took off my jewelry and put it in my bag, Win, lose or draw, I'm not afraid of what fate may have. At nine o'clock I didn't even run to my car, I walked extra slow to make sure he was never to far. I damn near waited for him to come out, we made eye contact, and not a word to his car he headed right out.

I don't go to work to fuck with people, but if you fuck with me, get ready to prove your my equal. I want to get along harmoniously. I guess that will be the difference between a wankster and a real bitch like me.

The End

STAGE PERFOR-MANCE

Alone

Your hands caress my thighs,
Stroking them so sensuously.
I fell the warmth of your breath,
On my navel.
As your lips gently glide past.
Your tongue takes a ride,
Across my breast.
And I can smell,
The sweet smell of baby oil,
On your breath,
That reminds me of the place,
You just left.
I wrap my fingers around your neck,
Pulling your lips close to mine.
Getting my body prepared,
For that all night grind.
I open my eyes.
Catch a glimpse of the candle lite.
I listen to the air,
And notice an absent tone.
That's when I realized.
I was all alone!

Kiss A Girl

Would you mind if I kiss a girl?
Oh I'm not gay.
Just curious,
The way her lips and tongue taste.
I'm curious to see,
If her pussy gets wetter than mine.
And if her thighs are as soft,
As that big behind.
Can you blame me for being greedy?
Look at her body,
So tight and so needy.
Oh but no I'm not greedy,
I'm going to let her tongue cascade,
Where ever it pleases me.
Grab her by the ears,
Hit her with slick line after slick line.
Imagine her back to you,
and my hips in a slow grind.
I think I'll let her go,
For an hour at a time.
Flip her over into a sixty-nine.
Chasing that pink pony,
Until the bitch says it mines.
Then together will cum,
Simultaneously with divine.
So,
Would you mind if I kiss a girl?
Oh, I'm not gay,
But right now I want to see.
How her lips and tongue taste.

Hard Ass Dick

There is nothing I love more than a hard ass dick.
Bigger than an atari joystick,
And if your game is tight you might watch my head dip.
They say us "Bama" girls give good brains.
And I love to slob on rock hard things.
I'll put that dick between my tits,
Look in your eyes as I tickle that slit.
Open up wide and touch the back of my throat.
With no gag reflex baby girl won't choke.
I promise I won't neglect your balls.
I'll hum like a vacuum as they enter my dental halls.
Oh yea the fun is about to begin.
I going to let you kiss my third eye,
Before you almost put it in.
See I just want to bob on top of that head,
and let you anticipate putting that hard as dick to bed.
Smack me, flip me, tie me down.
Pull my hair, call me a bitch right now.
Whore, slut words don't even matter.
Just serve me some hard ass dick on a silver platter.
And if you serve me with a whole bunch of class.
I'm going to turn around and let you put it in my ass.
Oh no, inside you won't cum.
I'm going to drop to me knees and get the job done.
So fella's if you want to see me spit.
Put your fist in the air,
And give me that hard ass dick.

Exhibitionist

I'm a exhibitionist, ex-a ex-a bitionist.
Exhibitionist, ex-a ex-a bitionist

Call me a poet lyricist.
As I exhibit all of this.
I'm not a narc so get addicted to me.
As I shoot these stanzas expeditiously.
See I'm the type of chick you all want to me.
I got my Trump on in public,
and Vanessa Del Rio between the sheets.
When I'm on this stage it's my alter ego you meet.
So let's go ahead and make this bitch complete. (Strip)

I'm a exhibitionist, ex-a ex-a bitionist.
Exhibitionist, ex-a ex-a bitionist.

Now I've got you hypnotized,
who shot ya between the eyes?
Hey honey,
Don't you dare blink.
Sweetie,
Don't you dare move,
Take this tube of lube,
because I'm about to show you my boobs.
Exhibit A (tits)
no fuck that exhibit B (ass)
and if your game is tight,

You might get exhibit C-U-N-T.

Because, I'm a
Exhibitionist, ex-a ex-a bitionist.
Exhibitionist, ex-a ex-a bitionist.

Call me the Beyonce of poetry.
Bringing sexy back narcissistically.
I'm going to shake my ass across this stage.
And pop my hips to every indecent phrase.
Hey fella's pass me a blunt.
Bitches go ahead and call me a cunt.
Unless your the type of chick whose mind is free as me.
Superman this poem (superman dance) expeditiously.

Because I'm a
Exhibitionist, ex-a ex-a bitionist.
Exhibitionist, ex-a ex-a bitionist.

I'm crazy in love with this stage.
And you got to admit,
My exhibit is a little insane.
By the end of this poem,
I'm going to have you saying my name.
Lenore,
Because you eyes are my paparazzi,
taking still images of me.
Hey baby lets go to the bathroom and play R-Kelly.
Except I'm the one that get's to pee!

Not guilty,
ex-a ex-a bitionist
Exhibitionist, ex-a ex-a bitionist.

Tonight,
I wasn't afraid to drop my dress.
I wasn't afraid to freak this poetry nest.
And I'll never be a size two,
And Bootylicious,
These Jackson's just don't do.
But,
My personality is off the charts.
And my stilettos,
Are leaving poetry skid marks.
When you came out tonight,
you didn't expect all of this.
But I'm about to walk off this stage,
And you're going to remember
That hard ass dick.
So the next time you hear,
Lenore's doing her poems.
Sit back and relax,
and let me get my exhibit on.

Because I'm a
Exhibitionist, ex-a ex-a bitionist,
Exhibitionist, ex-a ex-a bitionist.

TOXIC

This is round II on stage,
With a new book spelling my name.
"Infallible Love"
My love of poetry.
God's second chance,
Of following my dream.
Yet, my road was rocky,
Years ran swift like a stream.
My body was so toxic,
God knows what I mean.
I had to detox my body,
And detox my mind.
Change the way I think,
We only get one lifetime.
I'm Lenore the Poet,
And Rosalind's the debt collector.
Subliminally I kept telling her,
"Bitch we could do better!"

Plus Chasity's in my ear,
saying Lenore your a star,
You've got to admit I'm a little
Je ne sais quoi.
Meaning, I got that little something extra,
That makes you want to believe.
Love me or hate me,
Tonight you're here to see me.
This is my life, this is who I am.
I'm a woman,
That don't give a damn.
Poetry's my feast,
And my words are a beast.
None of that God-body shit,
Just simple like a crease.
I'm more than just sex on stage,
I'm a strong black woman,
Whose mind you will not play.
I've got book sense,
Common sense,
And soldiers that got my back.

I'm doing this like "Roca-Fella"
So I can watch my dough stack.
Because,
I detoxed my body,
And detoxed my mind.
L-e-n-o-r-e,
Spells,
Poetry hustling time.
Now I'm back on this poetry dream,
I'm about to break.
All I have to say is,
As-Salaam ailakum

LADIES
FIRST

SHUT UP!

Shut up,
About how fat you are,
Either love your curves,
Or work that blubber off.
Shut up,
Stop complaining you can't lose weight,
While you scarf down,
That second piece of cake.
Shut up,
Lying your a size ten.
When it's yeast infected jeans,
Your trying to squeeze in.
There is nothing wrong,
With being plus sized.
If you love yourself,
And your esteem is high.
I use to be a size 16,
But I wasn't happy.

I had to do,
What was best for me.
To stop feeling crappie.
No fad diet, No starvation,
No zone, or slim fast aggravation.
I got off the couch,
And took my fat ass to the gym.
Five days a week,
I worked my way slim.
Cardio, weights, boxing and pilates.
I only ate when I was hungry,
Naturally healthy to fuel my body.
So sista's stop complaining,
As you watch TV. and lay up,
Either do something about it,
or,
Just SHUT UP!

Black Woman Frown

Sista's why are you so mad?
Can life really be that bad?
All I see is black women frown.
All I see is black souls weighed down.
You have breath,
You have life,
You have so much to give.
You have hope,
You have dreams,
You have a reason to live.
So why must you take this undeniable stand?
Life is less complicated, if you stop worrying about a man.
Are you waiting to be swept off your feet?
You're waiting for a man, and still won't be complete.
That frown is deeper than the opposite sex.
That frown comes from your soul being perplexed.
You're jealous, judgmental, with a frown so visible.
You won't be happy until everyone is miserable.
The truth is you don't love yourself.
And why would a man want a woman with no wealth?
Not wealth of money, but wealth of soul.
The wealth of freedom only a smile beholds.
I want to take you by your shoulders,
And shake your mind free.
I want to smack you in your face saying,
Bitch............please!

And I'm not preaching to the choir.
I'm a sista whose soul has been re-wired.
There are so many women,
That love to smile like me.
Yet year by year,
We are becoming a dying breed.
As we watch our men,
Go off to White and Asian land.
Why should they put up,
With such a despicable stand?
A brother brought this to my attention to convey.
So as I go around,
I take a mental survey.
He was right,
All around town,
I see so many sista's with that,
Black Woman Frown.

Help

Lay on a couch,
And get your mind analyzed.
Maybe you will find,
You have more issues than mine.
There's nothing wrong,
With asking for help.
It's when you don't ask,
You play the hand you were dealt.
Many women have daddy issues,
Emotional trauma, and physical abuse.
You walk around,
Creating so much drama,
Then you wonder,
What is wrong with your Karma.
Pretending as if you on the earth.
But when your alone,
You realize you have no self worth.

I was lucky,
To have Sebastian tell me the truth,
His honesty helped me,
Heal my childhood abuse.
If God didn't send you a Sebastian,
Then take the matter in your own hands.
Admitting you are weak,
Is the fist step to becoming a woman.
I rather see,
More sista's in therapy,
Letting the emotional bonds of the past,
Just fry free.
If your not happy,
With the hand you were dealt.
Lay down on the couch,
And don't be afraid to ask for help.

Learn Who You Are Dealing With

I'm tired of bitches crying and spying.
Calling up "Cheaters," because their man is lying.
It's time you learn who you're dealing with,
Except for the hosts stabbing,
Your fame aint legit..
I fell in love with a hustler.
A pimping type of brother.
Most wanted in his game,
Plenty of bitches in ATL know his name.
But,
I know who I'm dealing with,
And monogamy aint at the top of my list.
Monogamy is becoming a thing of the past,
It slapped me in my face,
When my mother passed.
Don't get it twisted,
Because every man is not the same.
And with so many whores,
Few are making "M" their middle name.
Yet, If you have to call "cheaters",
Then it wasn't meant to be.
If you are sitting at home crying,
Then ask that bitch to leave.
So many women want love so bad,
They lead themselves,
Down the same punishing path.

You're sitting around miserable,
Until you pick up the phone.
Lights,
Camera,
Action,
Now you look pathetic and alone.
If you're dealing with a man,
who aint coming home.
He only texts you once a week,
And hard to reach on the phone.
If he calls you a relative,
to someone else on the other end,
He definitely not your man,
And probably barely a friend.
When he talks he always snap,
You're driving by his crib like it's the trap.
If he creeping out late at night.
And your waiting up until 6am to start a fight.
If you keep asking,
"God why is this happening to me."
You should be saying,
"Damn what is wrong with me."
So,
Then next time your desperate,
and start swaying your hips.
Before you open up wide,
Learn who you're dealing with.

I OBJECT!

I object to black women's
Personal judgment.
I don't need to hear stories,
On their insecure subjects.
It's usually the ones that are loud,
And want to be seen.
Who don't have a pot to piss in,
Just miserable and mean.
They judge others,
When it's truly them that are trife.
And they can't figure out why,
They live a lonely life.
Crazy is,
As Crazy does.
Truly they are missing,
A lot of self love.
I'm sure this applies
For other races too.

But I'm concerned with mine,
And the good nigga's we slowly lose.
I object,
To black women,
Whose minds are a mess.
Missing out on life,
Adding so much undue stress.
Right now,
My judgment is just conversation,
Bring to light a simple observation.
It should be a law,
To stamp their heads "Reject."
Until that is passed,
I just simply object.

Cater

This man shortage,
Got Sista's losing their mind.
Catering to men,
That aint even worth their time.
Of course you old whore's,
Are half dressed looking like dimes.
But next week,
The young sluts will take your place in line.
The, "I gotta have a man," women,
Make me sick.
Act like they would die,
If they lived life without a dick.
So desperate their standards are starting to slow.
Truth is their self esteem is really low.
Instead of building themselves up,
They rather put on a show.
Their package reads: play me,
All wrapped in a pretty bow.

There are so many races,
You should explore.
Please get your mind right first,
Or eventually they will walk out the door.
There really isn't a man shortage,
Just a lot of brothers in jail.
Yet,
I'm more concerned with my sista's,
Whose minds are locked,
In an invisible cell.
Instead of catering to these losers,
You should be catering to yourself.
Catering to your mind,
And your spiritual health.
When your broke and alone,
Trying to re-stack that paper,
Kudos, you got played.
Be careful to whom you cater.

It's Not About You

I hate bitches who think,
It's all about them.
Acting like they are God,
When they are only a part of his plan.
Bitch,
You're not the reason the sun came up.
The stars shine at night.
The beaches caress a beautiful tide.
Can you make a rain drop,
Fall from the sky?
Bitch,
You can wear all the,
Gucci, Target, or Marshalls you want.
Clothes will never give you,
as much money as Trump.
You can be "Halle" on the outside,
but you soul radiates,

the dark side.

Bitch,
It's not about you,
Your people let you get away with that shit,
But it's obvious you ain't ran across,
The right chick.
Talk crazy if you want,
You cant be saved,
By your Yves St. Laurent.
Bitch,
We look at you and laugh,
shaking our heads.
Because your the type of bitch,
That ends up dead.
So pathtic our hearts go out to you.
So lost people are laughing at,
But not with you.
So one day your gonna learn,
A lesson so true.
It's all about God,
And not about you.

"M's" Ether

Forgive me lord, Because I'm about to sin.
Unforseen circumstances,
Got me writing about this bitch again.
Old ass bitch, with a raggedy ass weave.
Fucked up skin,
And an attitude that man her man leave.
Aged, bitter and miserable,
Her job is her only escape.
Alone, lonely and phony,
Can't buy dick to participate.
Her strenght comes from being a snitch.
Instead her tongue rattled, like a weak bitch.
"Nique" cant you see you associate,
With Losers.
You're so much better than Gucci, Grey-
hound,
And emtional insecure abusers.
Plus her lies "fired" my folks.
Becareful old whore,

You could find yourself,
in a hold of choke.
I even aplogized to this bitch,
because I grew out of my childish shit.
Yet, she going to live miserable and trife.
Probably buy another title of wife.
I'm glad you stopped me from getting that
job.
You were afraid of the self esteem,
I would rob.
Had the nerve to comment,
On how much weight I lost.
Yet her eyes read, "I'll never be that hot."
Hi hater,
Thank you for keeping my dream alive.
Because each time you hate,
God bless me with more shine.
Don't ever think for a moment,
My poetry is a sleeper.
This is your second dedication,
I'm going to call it,
"M's" Ether.

Quit It: Book II

So I hear you claim,
I wrote a book about you.
Bitch,
Give me some credit,
I wrote two poems about stupid shit you do.
Since I didn't name names,
Only a dumb bitch would claim that fame.
Me and Daddy have a contest,
Hands off ways to make a bitch cry.
Now I'm one up,
So I must thank you,
For breaking that tie.
It was 2005 please move on.
As matter of fact keeping talking,
To you I dedicate this third poem.
Since,
This didn't cause you any shame,
Let me add a couple of more names.

Broke,
Baby making,
Slut,
You serve your pussy on a rusty platter.
Stank,
Tramp,
Jump off,
Whatever I call you really don't matter.
You fuck friends, co-workers,
Random nigga's on the street.
And when they are done,
They pass the baton like a track meet.
(Next)
You talked it up dear,
I'm making all your dreams come true.
I haven't seen in years,
but you made it,
Book II
(Quit It)

"A" To My Left

My corporate world turned upside down.
My girl "Adamville," had to turn debt collection down.
I'm happy for her opportunity,
My sister Taurus got the humor in me.
I don't go to work to make friends,
But once in a while.
Some are worth extending my hand.
The transition wouldn't be that bad.
If your replacement was a weird little lad.
I'm embarrassed he's a poet,
I may be wrong but is "crack" heroic?
Just when the team was starting to be OK.
A piece of my harmony is taken away.
Plus she loves Beyonce just as much as me.
Our last Hoorah,
Will be a concert a Phillips with "B."
Right now,
I'm stuck in captivity as I look to my left.
Maybe this weirdo will be OK.
Oh hell no,
I wish he would exit stage left.
My selfishness got me vexed.
And right now my left just got hexed.
Truth is,
I'm going to miss,
"A" to my left.

Dying Breed

A book signing for "Recently Divorced."
Strong Black women,
Showed up in force.
Store owner, film makers,
and publishers of course.
Real estate agents, singers and writers,
Came together with no remorse.
All black and beautiful to the eye.
Came in every color, shape and size.
Trading business cards no one was obsolete.
Sisters, supporting Sisters,
Sitting in peace to eat.
A room full of black women.
Trying to succeed.
A room full of black women
Who coat checked insecurities.
It could have been a catastrophe,
Instead it was the rebirth
Of a dying breed.

Ode 2 "B"

I admit it,
I'm a fan of "B"
She musically helped me,
Prepare for my destiny.
My psychologist told me,
I was depressed.
So when I'm feeling down,
Listen to something,
That will calm my unrest.
No, No, No, No, No,
Had me saying,
Yes, Yes, Yes, Yes, Yes.
The writing on the wall,
Read my life was a mess.
Mary-Alice had me,
Jumpin, Jumpin,
As I laid on her couch.
My childhood issues,
I began to forget about.
I was and independent survivor,
Putting on a happy face.
I was dangerously in love,
Felling like a hip hop star all over the place.
It was me, myself and I,
Crazy in love,
Catering to my own mind.

I had a solider on my hand,
Then through with love,
Became the game plan.
Yet,
I kept having De Ja Vue,
So,
I gave him the green light,
and to the left he could move.
Resentment,
My tears would cry,
Until I listened,
To the voice deep inside.
It's funny how I grew up with "B."
Except,
I'm 37 years old,
And unknowingly she shaped my destiny.
My future look bright,
As each year I behold.
This one is for "B,"
To you I present this ode.

It's My Fault

I admit it,
It's my fault.
I should have long walked away,
When you got caught.
Up,
In your issues.
I didn't care,
because I wasn't being misused.
Now our love is lost,
Because you value love much more,
when it comes at a cost.
I remember when you use to love me,
I never asked for anything.
So when you gave,
It was more than free.
I understood,
You lived by the streets.
Pimping aint easy,

And,
I'm not the average bitch you meet.
I let love blind me,
Hanging in years with you.
Yet,
My trust was being abused.
What I thought was love,
Each day became more confused.
Hoping one day you would change.
Until I realized that day never came.
I saw love in your eyes,
But our minds wasn't in sync
I take responsibility for everything,
I let you do.
And until this day you still don't have a clue.
Don't take this as an apology,
It's my way of moving past love psychology.
I had to bring all my feeling to a halt,
I admit it failed myself,
Because it's my fault.

Phenomenal Lenore

Phenomenal Lenore,
Trying so hard to hide.
Let other bitches,
Make me feel insecure,
On the inside.
Pehnomenal Lenore,
Use to hate herself.
Took responsibility for everyone,
Except myself.
Phenomenal Lenore,
Use to make bad decisions,
Could have ended up dead,
Or came up missing.
Phenomenal Lenore,
fell flat on her face,
dusted her self off,
And fell in love with her face.

I'm finally,
As Phenomenal as I want to be,
Confident, strong and secure,
And a hell of a personality.
A heart that endures,
Took a phenomenal leap of faith.
Gave it up to God,
Because in me,
He sees his face.

Phenomenally,
More than a sexy stride.

Phenomenally,
More than a sexy mind.

I'm,
Phenomenal Lenore,
Until the day I die

THE
MEN
ALL
PAUSED

Blind Hell Date

Six two, Chocolate, loving Ohio state.
Good conversation on the phone,
Damn could this be my new mate?
His first time out and about in ATL
His labels read broke,
And new conversations about his stint in jail.
Slowly this fantasy turned into a blind hell date.
His mind was still locked on his ex-cell mate.
He was afraid to live,
His conversations lived in the past.
Nothing to look forward to,
But a blunt and lifetime Marta pass.
I didn't like his negativity it started to bring me down.
He wanted to buy our drinks,
But I was going dutch right now.
Earlier, I didn't like the way he was eyeing my crib.
Talking about our next time,
But I'm sure by then my shit would have been his.
So, I sent him a subliminal message,
Letting him know my nine was in my purse.
Loaded the clip and cocked it back,
To let his mind play it in reverse.
He wasn't as smart as me, Nor the solider type.
So for the rest of the evening,
I'm looking for a light-skinned cutie I could swipe.
I even tried to push him on other chicks,

Suggesting lames that was more his speed.
No matter how hard I tried,
His focus kept coming back to me.
He was culturally missing,
All night gay men dissing.
So I decided to probe it a little more.
From what I could tell,
In jail his butt was probed sore.
He walked like his ass held a cock,
My body language read available.
In fear this undercover,
Would bring down my stock.
Four hours later my patience had disappeared.
This date was over,
But he wanted to go back upstairs.
I nipped that in the bud,
And pointed across at Marta over there.
He looked disappointed,
And figured out I wasn't his new mate,
I didn't give a damn,
I just wanted to end,
This blind hell date.

My Bad

Meet this nigga in Cumberland Mall streets
Kind of cute, and his gear was all right to me.
My freak inside was feeling true,
But I'm not the type to say I do.
Yet, I had some time to waste,
I caught him with a wink,
And a sexy turn of my face.
One look in my eyes,
And this nigga couldn't turn away.
I gave him my number,
And dashed on my merry way.
2 hours later "609" rings my phone.
All I heard,
Was Blah blah at the other end of the phone.
"609", I've got to hit you back.
Nah, not really because his personality was wack.
9 P.M. I'm texting daddy,
As I'm rolling a blunt.
"609" rings my phone,
It must be voice mail that he wants.
2 days later,
Me and daddy balling out,
Here come "609" doing the voice mail count.
Damn can this nigga take a hint?
Not calling him back,
Isn't it evident?

Next day at work,
I'm trying to get paid.
I get two more calls,
Now I'm about to make this nigga's day.
Plus this nigga got me mistook.
I text him

"You're acting desperate and that's not a good look."

He answers me back with this exact plea.

"What kind of tactics you using, you approached me?"

The devil on my shoulder,
Is saying take this marks dough.
But the angel on the other is saying,
He's going to make it hard,
When it's time for him to go.
Yet,
He deserves an answer,
Because that was pathetic and sad.
All I could text him back.

"My bad."

Light Skinned Cutie

Light skinned cutie,
It's something about the contrast of our skin.
That makes me sweat so deep within.
The red ones,
On a bad day will do.
But they must have swagger,
And be hella cute,
The yellow ones,
Can tickle my throttle.
But their aint nothing like,
My daddy mulatto's.
And they are becoming a dying breed.
I'm trying to bring them back Atlanta,
But fellas,
A little help please.
The shortage got the chocolate,
changing my mind.
Nah, they can be eye candy,
And rub on my thigh.

Back to the matter at hand,
I want to give a shout out,
To all the light skinned men.
I'm gonna start a website,
Called light skinned cutie.com
Please email your reservations,
And your ass better be the bomb.
Don't get it twisted,
Your color won't get you past the velvet rope.
Your mental have to be,
Full of life and a whole lot of hope.
Dress like a star with his mind on the streets.
Keep my freak secrets between the sheets.
No fake as gangsters need to apply.
I need a light skinned brother,
Ready to ride or die.
So If you know your a thoroughbred,
Then baby I want to be your department head.
As a chocolate sister it's my duty,
To bring back,
The light skinned cutie.

Sex In The City

Strolling thru "tar-jay," (target)
Passing the lunch time,
Part of the day.
Just happen to have,
My stilettos on,
But still professional,
To the bone.
Then I hear,

"Excuse me miss, you have beautiful shoes."
"And with legs like those you can't lose."

Then,
He asked to take a picture of my feet.
Sure I replied,
If this is what makes you complete.
Out comes the digital camera.
He bends close to the floor.
Snap, Snap, Snap,

Hold up,
I'm going to charge you,
If you take anymore.
He looked up calm and relaxed.
As if he just came.

"One more question please."

So I gave him a fake name.
Dude wants to take me shopping,
and I only have to let him put them on.
Whitey must be crazy,
It's sounding like a murder about to go
wrong.
I looked at him and smiled,
With eyes full of pity,
Nigga,
Who do you think I am?
"Charlotte," from sex in the city.

I Need

I need someone who accept my excuses,
On why I'm not there.
Or begin to choke when he lies,
As if he grasping on air.
I need someone,
Who doesn't want to be everyone's friend.
Who will put me first,
And worry about everyone else in the end.
Someone who understands,
That I need my space,
And don't use my space,
Like pimp trying to trump my ace.
I need someone,
Who believes and accepts my dream.
Stand by me when I'm down,
And not when the money starts to stream.
I need someone,

That when I call,
Will come and tame my freak.
Not at his priority,
During the middle of the week.
I need someone,
Who's game is a slick as his dick.
And not get mad,
When it's my own game I start to spit.
I need a man,
Who can play me in chess.
The only type,
That understands a mind so complex.
Honesty,
Wisdom,
And knowledge he will feed.
This is the type of man,
That I need.

Almost Famous
(ode 2 Ed)

Some think I failed,
For following my dream.
Yet,
I was so happy,
God put that faith in me.
I can't let Ed's toast go to waste,
Almost famous,
Three glasses,
And Vue to taste.
When I raised my glass,
My first book was done.
Yet I questioned,
Would it become number one.
Now I know it was only a test.
I gave up to early so God put it to rest.
Back into the world in which I ran away.
Calling people for their bills to pay.

I put away my paper and pen,
gave up on my dream deep within.
I let my dream die,
As poetry nights began to fly by.
I asked?
Was I really afraid to fail,
Is that why I didn't succeed.
Because if I wasn't afraid of failure.
My dream wouldn't escaped me.
Chastity kept tell me,
I had what it takes to be a star.
But In my mind, The dream had fallen to far.
Ed's toast kept ringing in my mind.
Would it be arrogant,
For it to be the title next time?
Is It really about the money and fame?
Or is it my history I'm trying to reclaim?
Trying this shit again,
Could be financially dangerous.
But from the mouth of Ed,
I'm almost famous.

Ring The Alarm

Ring the alarm,
I've been through this to long,
I'm ready to see,
Another chick on your arm.
I'm going to be rocking,
My un-cloudy stones,
Jimmy Choo shoes,
Driving my lexus coop,
And the nigga next to me,
Won't be you.
You pronounced your love for me,
Like a wolf hollers at the moon.
Yet when shit went awry,
Your love left to soon.
I wonder if your love,
Was only a front,
Or was it the good head,
That you want.
Back forth, forth and back

The shit became wack.
I understand that your a pimp,
And like a real hustler,
You couldn't go out like a whimp.
If my first book was a success,
I'm sure by my side you would have blessed.
I'm so glad I see the real you,
Because a half-baked pimp just wont do.
Plus your friends began to show disrespect,
Sooner or later you would have been next.
Blah, Blah, Blah,
Each word was a lie,
I'm fucking glad we severed our ties.
Dumb bitches want to pay,
To buy your love,
I refused to pay for what's been used up.
That's why,
I'm ringing the alarm,
I've been through this too long.
I'm ready to see another chick on your arm.

Dear Korey

Dear Korey,
My one and only seed.
Only wanted the best for you,
So you would succeed.
I never gave you up,
I just gave you my best.
At 22, my mind was a mess,
You filled grandma's empty nest,
When her soul got tired,
We laid her to rest.
Through me God sent you,
To be in her life.
Because without you,
There would have been too much strife.
It hurt grand-dad when I took you away.
But his decisions weren't right,
So I couldn't let you stay.
There's a reason me and your father,
Don't have much to say,
When we were together,

I had hell to pay.
Even though his life appears stable.
I'm going to teach you,
What he isn't able.
Father and step-mom,
Thinks I'm trying to buy your love.
Yet, you won't grow up lame,
Like he was.
I'm about to fill your life with joy.
Expensive toys for my baby boy.
The best education where you can dream.
I say "O-State," but that's not up to me.
You're a star on field with a lot of esteem.
Ohio breeds champions on their football
team.
At 37, I'm proof people can change,
I didn't escape in "92,"
My life wouldn't be the same.
In the end I'm going to write our story.
My one and only seed,
My dear Korey.

Dear Daddy,

Dear daddy,
I'm sorry I didn't trust myself.
I knew that gold digger,
Was bad for your health.
Your death left me wounded inside.
Yet,
I was already prepared for your demise.
Your funeral was as fake as can be.
You deserve much more humanity.
You were a solider in more ways than one.
Uncle SAM couldn't do it,
So the devil got the job done.
You were my protector,
My benefactor,
And my best friend.
I've turned hard on the inside.
And like you,
Keep my gun close to my hand.
Damn,

Why did she let you slip away.
She never called 911,
And God is going to make her pay.
But I blame myself,
For not protecting my number one man.
I should have fought you,
Every step of the way.
Because,
Her eyes read insurance pay day.
You found her in the projects,
Where my grandma died.
And I wonder if you left her there,
Would you still be alive.
She is caught in Lucifers cell,
And her redemption is waiting in hell.
Right now I'm sad,
But each day I'm relearning to be happy.
I dedicate this poem.
To my beautiful daddy.

My Son

Heartache and heart break,
Weigh down on me like a ton.
But,
I'll never love any man,
The way I love my son.
When I was young.
My mind was all a twist.
His fathers reign.
Pounded,
Like an iron fist.
I was selfish and lost,
Living my life wild.
Definitely not a woman,
Ready for a child.
I loved you so much,
To Roy and Peggy,
I gave you up.
Now they are both gone.

He's with his father,
and so called step mom.
Although years later,
His father has changed.
I still to this day wish,
I never signed my name.
So many have tried,
But my son is not a pawn.
Nothing can break,
The womb in which we bond.
He understands why we aren't together.
Our love can withstand any weather.
I'm the one keeping his gear tight.
I'm the reason his pockets stay right.
I'm finally a woman,
And life without him isn't much fun,
But I'll never love any man.
The way I love,
My son.

God
Is
Telling
Me
Something!

Reasonable Doubts

I got reasonable doubts
On my next thing,
Stepping out on a poetry,
sex swing.
I prefer to rehearse,
My life in each verse.
But when I'm up on stage,
I get standing ovations,
for my sex rage.
Of course my doubts are reasonable.
Because when it's over,
Next comes judgment day.
And I don't want to blur that cloud,
With promiscuous shades of grey.
Yet,
He keeps sending me a sign.
Fade to black,
And your star will shine.
I'm using sex,
To get the worlds attention.

And my ultimate plan,
Is a young women's intervention.
Clear all the doubts,
They have in their mind.
Lift them up to a world,
So cold and so blind.
Show them every situation has a reason.
And don't get lost in youthful treason.
I'm ready for the nay slayers and poet haters,
No time to worry about unsuccessful traitors.
I have reasonable doubts,
But am I suppose to take a different route?
Ignore who I am,
Worry about the next man.
No,
I'm moving forward with this dream.
Because the words I write are extreme.
I can never be excused of being fake.
And God's love I will never forsake.
Like frost on my car isn't unseasonable.
And my doubts aren't unreasonable.

Chapter One

A new chapter in my life is about to begin.
I found out the hard way,
God's my only true friend.
Sitting in my crib 20 stories above,
And the lights of Atlanta,
Hasn't shown me any love.
Why is it only pain in my life,
That helps me write?
Looking at the Coca-Cola building,
Saying this can't be life.
Living between two on-ways.
West Peachtree and Spring.
In either direction I could be a queen.
One way takes me to debt collecting,
The other is a poets blessing.
But I'm sitting in my window,
On a Friday night.
Looking up Spring a poets delight.
Yet W. Peachtree has me in a corporate trap.

I need money to do this book,
So that lick keeps me going back.
Six days a week, overtime at it's peak.
I'm so unhappy it leave me poetically weak.
Yet,
It all became an excuse.
Because the first book I paid no dues.
Stock option afforded a life that pleased.
I partied away my marketing fees.
Maybe it wasn't my time,
But a test from A God so divine.
He wasn't going to just let,
The door open for me,
I had to work hard,
Like when Moses parted the sea.
Playing the victim,
Will never get this book done.
Spring street is the start,
Of a new chapter one.

Testify

I must testify,
Because God sealed it in my mind.
I'm on a challenge,
That could alter my life line.
I woke up Sunday morning,
With very little sleep.
He led me to Decatur,
Where his roots are steep.
I flew away with the choir,
Harmoniously they set me on fire.
I read responsively,
To John 3:17.
The Great Jerry Black,
Preached Samuels 1-7-3.
I looked over the balcony,
And closed my eyes in prayer.
It definitely wasn't a dream,
But I was no longer there.
I was at a concert,

Couldn't see who was on stage.
The heavens opened up,
And Gods hand gave way.
I kept jumping and reaching,
Trying to Grab his hand.
He wasn't making it easy,
For me to reach his promise land.
All of the sudden,
He picked me up,
And placed me on stage.
Turned me around,
And it was me the crowd praised.
He enlightened me so much,
I almost fell of the pew.
The church lady beside me,
Gave me a look of,
"What is wrong with you?"
All I have to do is jump and try,
And only through my poems,
He allows me to testify.

Soul Cleansing

It's time I cleanse my soul, Of all the bad
things,
That has stopped my flow.
My past issues are haunting me.
In my dreams,
The devil effects me unconsciously.
The only way to get him of my back.
Is to cleanse my soul and never look back.
Who was the little girl?
Ridiculed because of her nappy curls.
Skin so dark it made her hurl.
Who was the latch key kid, Abused by a fa-
miliar kid.
Could this have been the start,
Where her personality hid?
The outcast of the basketball team.
Shot the wrong way, paper started to ream.
In high school she wanted to be popular,
Instead the popular laughed at her,
When they passed her locker.

Suicide attempt at Alabama A&M.
A cry for help when domestic abuse began.
Carrying his child,
Baby Daddy knocking her down.
Pushing her self esteem no where to be found.
She had the guts to walk out on the abuse.
But all of this left too many issues.
Living in Atlanta,
Saw a woman nearly beaten to death.
She couldn't take any more,
So insecurity had to move stage left.
Had a nigga playing her to the left,
It didn't matter was his fool every night.
It was time to kill this girl off.
She paid every lesson with a cost.
I'm so happy that she is dead.
And this paper has cleared my head.
Because the woman I've become,
Is a top class pedigree.
And the devil can move on,
Because my soul is clean.

Church Sinner

People are trying to force me,
To a join a church.
What they don't know,
I'm already doing the lords work.
I may curse and carry a gun.
Smoke weed,
And lust after the light skinned ones.
I may go out and party at night.
I may wear an outfit,
That hugs my body tight.
I may have sex without a ring.
I may be a freak,
Living out my sexual dreams.
I may love to shop,
And hear the sound of popping tags.
But I do go to work,
And pay for everything I have.
Sometimes I'm loud and a litle stearn.
Sometimes I demanding,
But still willing to learn.

I still pray each and every night.
I turn to God when something aint right.
I talk to him any time of the day.
And I help any man he sends my way.
Now this sinner isn't afraid to die.
This sinner will look God in the eye.
This sinner will repent all her sins.
This sinner will be walking into heaven.
I can admit that I'm not perfect,
And I do sin.
It's church folk that look at me,
As if only they know him.
It's the church sinners,
Those who are hypocrites,
"O praise the lord."
But still doing wicked shit.
There will come a day,
I will join a church.
I'll be baptized in the waters,
As a renewed winner.
The one thing I won't be,
Is a Church sinner.

Change

I know my change will come.
With God's blessings,
I'm a chosen one.
He looks past all the bad words,
It's only alphabets,
He's already heard.
I'm a child of God,
More than an empty soul,
In this "Bod."
My change doesn't depend on the next man.
My spiritual self,
Says I know I can.
Only God knows,
How far I've come.
And Satan is mad,
He lost this one.
I didn't have to sit in church,
To learn his word.

Via Television,
Reverend J. Black kept me alert.
He preached,
More than a coming of wealth.
He helped heal,
My spiritual health.
I love to party and have fun.
And sometimes it take a blunt.
To get the job done.
Some Christians may call me a heathen.
But I bet on God,
And always come up even.
I know sometimes,
I aint living right.
Even when I'm drunk,
I pray each and every night.
No one is perfect,
And we're not all the same.
I just thank God,
For the way I've changed.

God's Apology

I owe God and apology,
Even when I'm wicked,
He continues to bless me.
I kneel every night,
And the "Lords Prayer," I repeat.
I poor out my soul to a God I can't see.
I wonder if he's getting tired of lame excuses.
Letting my poetry become useless.
Yet each day he wakes me up,
Giving me another chance.
A decision to be happy,
Or the same debt collecting dance.
I'm so sorry God,
Because I'm finally sick and tired.
Nor will I let my poetry expire.
So Please,
Continue to acknowledge me.
Dear God,
This is my Apology

Lord Give Me A Sign

Lord give me a sign,
This gift aint hard to find,
I know it's my moment in time.
Lord give me a sign, I'm not ready to die
Stay in this crib and hide.
Lord give me a sign. I know my life is
blessed,
There's more than my material nest.
Lord give me a sign,
Please help my dream come alive,
Not only when I sleep at night.
lord gave me a sign,
I put this pen to the side & stepped outside.
Lord gave me a sign,
I was looking a mess,
Ran into Andre 3000 at CVS.
Put my book in his hand, another blessed
man.
Lord gave me a sign.

I Was- I Am

I was lost,
I was mean.
I was ugly on the inside,
And out.
I was confused,
I was dumb,
I was woman God lived without.
I thought it made me better,
To put others down.
I thought it made me better,
To see others frown.
I had more issues no doubt,
But my mind,
Couldnt figure them out.
Truth is,
I shouldn't have gave a fuck,
But my negativity,
Brought me nothing but bad luck

It hurt to find,
Friends became a victim,
Of my spite.
It was more than Karma,
I was a woman,
Living for drama.
I aplogize to some of the victims,
Of my first book.
Now I'm over myself,
I realized it wasn't a good look.
Growth is such a beautiful thing.
No longer a caged bird,
Who couldnt sing.
I'm not perfect by any means,
Nor am I throwing smoke screens.
I am found,
I am sound,
It took awhile,
To turn my life around.
I am better than I was.
Therefore I am.

Lenore

Rosalind is the name given as a child.
Lenore is the woman reborn to me now,
Rosalind was naive, ugly and mean.
A silly little girl with no self esteem.
Dying on the inside,
Living everyday as a lie.
Kept running in her dreams.
Afraid to look behind,
No where in sight was the finish line.
Until she awoke one day,
Confused and paralyzed.
Couldn't move her body,
Fear read in her eyes.
Each breath hurt as she tried to speak.
The devils web,
Had her vulnerable and weak.
"Our Father which are in heaven...."
She struggled to call out to the lord,
A flash of light appeared

And an angel guided with a silver sword.
She awoke and rose out of a cold sweat,
A dream of paralysis felt like death.
She dropped to her knees,
Began to pray for all her bad deeds.
She began to pray,
Morning, noon and night.
When her mind slipped,
She went back to gods right.
Shoulders back, head up,
Never looking at the ground.
When she got to cocky,
God put her on solid ground.
She had a purpose and a mission,
Lenore took over with all the ammunition.
Lenore's the one who steps on stage,
She took over and life became OK.
Sometimes Rosalind wants to step outside.
But Lenore's the one,
That keeps that bitch in line.

WHO, WHAT, WHERE, WHEN, AND WHY?

Star Dreams

I'm not a psychic,
But I see things in my dreams.
Some aren't perfect,
Most are hard to interpret.
They come backwards,
With no clues.
Yet,
Eventually some of them come true.
I love it when I lucid dream.
And If you have them,
You know what I mean.
When I'm lucid,
I love every opportunity.
Shed my inhibitions,
Acting like everything is new to me.
Now,
I always dream about,
One particular star.

I don't want to say his name,
Because I don't want to jinx that fast car.
Every time he comes to me,
He never brings any pain.
Instead in my pockets,
He makes it rain.
I wonder if the stars I see while I dream,
Is an illusion.
For what it really means?
Because,
I saw my fathers death
Two years before it happen.
Could I have saved him before he left.
I blame myself for his eternal sleep.
Now I can't change he's six feet deep.
What I see is more than fate,
It becomes reality,
If I'm patient and wait.
I may not understand what they mean,
Yet I'm not ready,
To jinx my star dreams.

Homeless

You can call me a bleeding heart.
And for some,
I wear my heart on my sleeve.
I will always help the homeless,
God places within my reach.
Today,
I gave a woman my vintage wool coat.
Straight off my back,
Because God wasn't going to let me feel
cold.
Some Friends turn a blind eye,
To the homeless clan.
They rather curse them out,
Then lend them a helping hand.
You can't help every body,
But feel a Soul that God embodies.
There's one homeless man on Cheshire
Bridge,
For Ten plus years he's walked that skid.
Inside Mcdonald's,
The Mexicans tried to shoo him away.

I stopped them,
And brought him a value meal that day.
The look in his eyes,
I knew God was present inside.
His thank you wasn't needed,
Because for him my soul had cried.
I walked to my car and let out a sigh,
When I looked back,
He was at the door waving Good bye.
If I ever get money I know what I have to do.
A philanthropist for the homeless,
And a place for troubled youth.
How can a country so rich,
Let Veterans, single mothers,
And teens sleep in a ditch.
I know my purpose on this earth,
Is to entertain and rejoice my birth.
Until the day comes,
When I can seal my creed.
For the homeless,
My heart will always bleed.

Pep Boys

The books I have read,
Helped shaped my mind.
And this time Pep Boys,
Fucked with the wrong dime.
Sun Tzu taught me,
"The Art Of War."
I taught myself to play chess,
So Pep Boys,
Became my checkmate whore.
"An Open Heart," The Dalai Lama,
Kept me Patient.
"Monster Kody Scott,"
Taught me when to make a statement.
So,
My "Rose Grew From The Concrete."
As months went on,

"E.A.R.L,"
Started to come out of me.
In the end,
"My Eyes Were Watching God."
I stood so firm,
That while "On A Move,"
Even Mumia Abu Jamal would applaud.
My car became,
"Life And Def,"
While in Pep Boys hands.
It was "Unbelievable,"
Like Biggies last stand.
Obey the Ten Commandments,
or you will feel the pain.
"The Purpose Of My Driven Life,"
Had their cash register opening,
And making it rain.

Chrysler Sucks

Let them "Nigga's" file bankruptcy,
Why should my tax dollars bail them out.
I bought one of their cars,
Now I'm on the same route.
Millions of dollars,
Isn't going to change their ways.
It's a "Ponzi,"
So the executives can get paid.
My LHS is pretty,
But falling apart with a cost,
Driving down 75
The decoration started blowing off.
The drivers side window,
Won't roll down.
The plastic in the back,
Is starting to peel around.
Lights flick,
On and off by it's self.

Starter,
Water Pump,
Head gasket,
And a timing belt.
Sludge in the engine,
Water and oil wont stop the mix.
Really,
They should give me the money.
So I can get this bitch fixed.
The government just extended their life,
As my tax dollars took a hike.
Run citizens run,
From the American made car.
If you understand what I'm saying,
Come have a drink at the bar.
We know the whole industry is corrupt.
I had to learn it personally,
That,
CHRYSLER SUCKS!

Real Housewives of the ATL?

The only thing real,
About a couple of these bitches,
Is their bank account.
But their attitude,
Voids those blank checks right out.
One of these chicks,
Got me ashamed of being black.
Even worse,
They are making the ATL look like crap.
B-R-A-V-O!
Got a few putting on,
A step and fetch show.
I love the broads in the O.C.,
Where it's sunny.
They aren't acting like niggas,
With brand new money.
New York kept it grimy,
Those chicks were,
Making moves and lots of cake.

I could never be jealous,
Of Atlanta's future ex-mates.
Like I said,
A couple of them are real.
The one's not trying to show off,
Their settlement deal.
Even the loud one seems mad cool,
Until she starts talking about her money.
My favorite is Keith's ex,
Baby girl is definitely no dummy.
However,
You're either born black or white,
There's no secret code on the inside.
Kissing ass,
Is never going make you do or die.
I hope it get's better,
Because right now we're looking like hell,
Come on Bravo,
These can't be,
The Real Housewives of the ATL?

Radio Air Play

I was a star today,
It was my first radio air play.
Easy rent a car sucks,
The chick at budget knew what was up.
One phone call,
And Roy beamed me to Enterprise.
Without my fathers faith,
My journey was about to subside.
The Nigerian in the shuttle,
Put a fist up for my cause.
Reminding me to stay focus,
Through the fog.
It was 85 south, Destiny and Street Disciples.
The world aligned during "99 Problems."
I was speeding,
And a trooper decided to solve them.
Thank you God,
For giving me big tits.
Propped up high and radio air play I had to spit.
I promised I would shout him out,
If he let me off.
He had a thing for sisters,
So the man let me drive off.
Driving through Alabama State,
The school looked the same.
Except I walked across campus,

Like a star looking for fame.
My best friend and high school sweetie,
Awaited at the radio station.
My womanly growth,
Had him figuring new conversations.
Then my mother stepped inside,
It was her twin,
Representing family pride.
I swear I was looking in Peggy's eyes.
She was there because it turned cold inside.
During the interview,
I turned on like a switch,
Me and Erica Fox talked and clicked.
It was good to be back home,
But I couldn't leave,
Without kissing my Daddy's dome.
327 miles from city to city.
I notice the lights of Atlanta,
Were more than pretty.
I spoke to strangers,
As Marta zipped me home.
Compliments from the ATL-iens.
I finally had a place to call my own.
I felt like a star,
On one long and exhausting day.
And a fire burned inside of me,
For more radio air play.

37

Tomorrow,
I turn 37,
And I feel as if,
I'm floating in heaven.
Yet,
Gas prices are high.
We send our men,
To Iraq to die.
Global warming,
Is creeping within time.
And criminals,
Are losing their fucking minds.
Paparazzi,
Has become a business.
Sub prime loans,
Are losing interest.
Bush is driving us,
Into debt.

I guess the stock market,
Will fall next.
Videos are no longer,
A technicality,
MTV has become all reality.
BET has cease to exist.
Keyshia is all I would miss.
The internet has become,
A way to reside.
People blog,
Instead of going outside.
Years ago,
I use to go to free concerts in the park.
Now,
It's only movies after the dark.
Vick should have fought dogs in ATL.
There are no laws,
So he wouldn't have went to jail.
Got myself a legal gun.
Now I want more than one.
This world is full of hate.
Hope I get to see 38.

Cloves

I'm killing myself,
With every puff I take.
These damn cloves,
Got me,
Spending five dollars a day.
Wake up coughing,
From the crap in my lungs.
It I really loved myself,
These cloves would be gone.
It's not scientific,
You don't need a degree,
To realize smoking is addictive.
People are dying everyday.
Yet,
I still puff,
My life away.
I'm stuck,
In an emotional place,
I don't want to be.

So I escape,
Filling my lungs with a nicotine sea.
I'm slowly drowning,
In a cloud of smoke.
I love the "truth," commercials,
As I puff, laugh, and choke.
Yet,
Cancer isn't funny.
Nor dying cancerous and broke.
Tobacco companies,
Don't want me to quit.
Because if I did,
The truth would be legit.
In my later years,
I want to be smoke free.
I want to put these cloves down,
And become,
A recreational smoker of weed.

Natural High

I'm on a natural high.
The kind of high a dub can't buy.
The fiends could sweep the streets all night.
Still couldn't inject what I feel inside.
One snort of the whitest snow,
Couldn't beat my natural blow.
"X" can make you shake your pants.
Except my high is saving the last dance.
Crack can leave you poor and broke.
What I got is wrapped in quotes.
Acid can have you seeing things.
What I got is better than fake dreams.
"GHB" can render you comatose.
However,
My high keeps me naturally afloat.
My high is about life.
Naturally blessed loved and bright!

I Miss You

I didn't want to write this poem,
Because it's going to tell how I really feel.
But after the day I've had,
I need to feel something real.
I'm around insecure women all day.
For whatever reason,
The thought of you make the drama go away.
I hate to admit,
We are connected through our soul.
But this back and forth love,
Is starting to get old.
I miss the way,
We stare into each others eyes.
I miss the way,
Our eyes get lost in others mind.
In the club we have no inhibitions,
We do what we want,
As if the crowd came up missing.

We bounce and freak each other,
Like the dirty south.
Throwing drinks in the air,
Until we are told to put the blunt out.
People see we're together,
When we walk through the door.
Step away, handle business,
Meet up and party so more.
I just paused,
And thought about my issue.
It's not these insecure bitches,
I realized,
I fucking miss you!

Today is December 25th, 2009, and I'm about to e-mail the final proof to my publisher. I felt the need to write this page since it's so ironic that I finished the first draft of my book a year ago to the exact day. My goal was to have this book done by the fall of 2009 with copies in hand, but as I stated in the beginning you can't pause life.

Winter has crept up on me quicker than I thought. The process of self publishing is not easy. Trying to get money together to pay the publisher in this recession was crazy. Plus my idea for the book party requires stage out fits, microphones, and practicing my ass off, has left me exhausted and I can't wait until I hit the stage in 2010. God has a plan for all of us, and I think this was the year I can say as an adult, I'm complete. I'm so normal that I just might be crazy!

THE END

It's done. I can't believe for the second time I just made my dream come true. I have no idea if this book will be a success However,it is a success because I brought my art to life.I hope I get a chance to do a third book. Because when I'm writing, and creating, it's when I'm at my best. Thank you all for being my friends, my associates, hell even my enemies. I hope one day I can add fans tothat list. Remember God loves us sinners to! Love Lenore

COVER PHOTOGRAPHER
SEBASTIAN@ INFINITE POSSIBILITIES

RIP EARL GRANT, YOU WILL BE MISSED!